Lettering Charts

FOR STUDENTS AND ARTISTS

PHYLLIS BROWN

Revised Edition

ANGUS & ROBERTSON PUBLISHERS

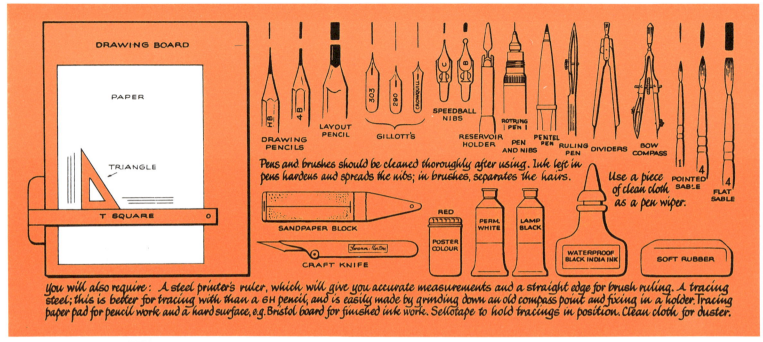

ANGUS & ROBERTSON PUBLISHERS

Unit 4, Eden Park, 31 Waterloo Road,
North Ryde, NSW, Australia 2113, and
16 Golden Square, London W1R 4BN,
United Kingdom

This book is copyright.
Apart from any fair dealing for the
purposes of private study, research,
criticism or review, as permitted
under the Copyright Act, no part may
be reproduced by any process without
written permission. Inquiries should
be addressed to the publishers.

First published in Australia
by Angus & Robertson Publishers in 1960
This revised edition first published in the United Kingdom
by Angus & Robertson (UK) Ltd in 1982
This revised edition 1977
Reprinted 1979, 1981, 1982, 1983, 1985 (twice)

Copyright © Phyllis Brown 1960, 1967, 1977

ISBN 0 207 13594 0

Printed in Shenzhen, China

DRAWING HINTS

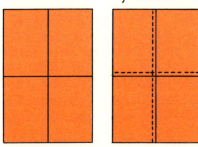

Actual Centre / *Optical Centre*

The optical centre is slightly above and to the left of the actual centre.

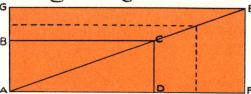

Scaling. To enlarge or reduce areas

To enlarge small area draw a diagonal A-C-E. Extend the base line A-D to desired length (F) and erect a perpendicular. Where this line cuts the diagonal (E) will be the required height. Reverse process to reduce.

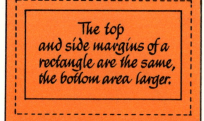

Margins

The top and side margins of a rectangle are the same, the bottom area larger.

The dotted line indicates a mechanical margin, all 4 sides equal.

PENCIL RENDERING

When doing pencil indications it is important to keep the tone even. Practise on Bond paper. Lightly indicate the letters first with a pointed pencil, then stroke in with a soft 4B pencil rubbed to a chisel edge on a sandpaper block. Practise the basic strokes first. Commence with Condensed Capitals 1" high, then do them in smaller sizes. Work with 2 pencils.

IAEOOSS CONDENSED letters NORMAL

EXPANDED SQUARE SERIFS

AOSZIII ROMAN letters

Italic Letters *Formal Script*

FREE STYLE *FREE STYLE*

BRUSH CONTROL

The Brush — a flat sable, size 4 or 5

Chisel edge — Round ferrule

HOW TO HOLD THE BRUSH

It is held between the thumb and first finger, firmly but lightly and does not touch the second finger. The three fingers underneath act as a bridge or rest, steadying the thumb and forefinger, yet leaving them free to manipulate the brush as the arm and hand slide up and down the paper. Relax the hand, never grip or pinch the brush.

HOW TO ROLL THE BRUSH FOR CURVED STROKES

Note thumb position at finish of strokes

TO ROLL BRUSH RIGHT

Hold the brush in an upright position. Now with your forefinger supplying all the action ROLL the brush BACK TOWARDS THE HAND. The brush will roll along the surface of the thumb. Lift gently towards finish.

TO ROLL BRUSH LEFT

Reverse the action and ROLL the brush in the opposite direction AWAY FROM YOUR HAND. It will still roll along the surface of the thumb propelled by the forefinger. Keep a steady, even pressure.

Holding the brush in the manner indicated practise the following strokes until you feel control of the brush. Only practice will give you this control. When you can do the strokes well, join them and do letters. Practise on newspaper using the column widths for guide lines; keep the strokes about 1" high. Use paint which must flow freely from the brush.

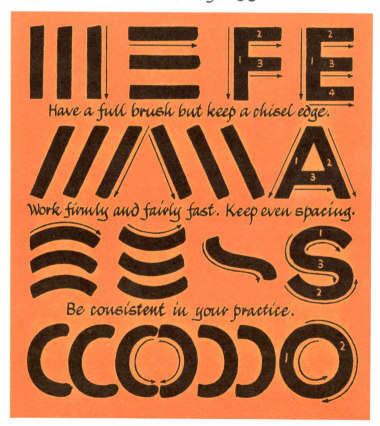

Have a full brush but keep a chisel edge.

Work firmly and fairly fast. Keep even spacing.

Be consistent in your practice.

If you find you are gripping the brush, stop and relax.

BRUSH BLOCK LETTERS

Practise these letters in Pencil first till you know the order of the strokes - then Brush on Newspaper - 1" letters.

Arrows indicate direction of the strokes - the chisel edge of the brush gives the clean finish to the ends. Train the eye as well as the hand and keep the letters upright and even in height and weight.

For Pencil practice use a 3B - rub the lead down to a chisel edge on a sandpaper block - make ½" letters.

SPACING (1)

Spacing is governed by Optical Illusions. (1) The letters must appear the same in weight; be uniform. (2) The white spaces between the letters must appear the same, and Blacks (letters) must balance Whites (spaces).

OPTICAL ILLUSIONS ENFORCE CERTAIN BASIC RULES

The eye sees horizontals thicker than perpendiculars. Rule: Horizontals must be a shade thinner and crossbars must be above centre, otherwise they appear to sag.
× Diagonals also appear thicker unless drawn thinner.

Circular masses appear smaller than rectangular masses. Rule: Curves must run slightly over the top or base lines, and the widest part of the curve must be drawn slightly wider than the perpendicular.

Angle letters appear shorter unless the points are extended. Rule: All letters ending in a point must have the point extended slightly over the top or base line.

* When spacing thin and thick letters, those with hairline sides must be placed a fraction closer together. The serifs on angle letters may overlap.

Letters are not the same in width, nor can they be spaced equal distances apart. Rule: Vertical sides need air and are spaced farthest apart. Round letters have to be closer together and angle letters may overlap.

Watch these letter combinations △ especially open letters. Adjust spacing by shortening serifs and horizontals.

HN IO ICA OO AV △ LA TY LT

SPACING (2)

Study the word, note verticals & open letters. Lightly pencil in letters – correct spacing – redraw carefully.

Incorrect
SPACING
Badly proportioned letters and spacing cause uneven balance of colour: holes and dark masses.

Incorrect
SPACING
Well-proportioned letters but mechanical, even, spacing has destroyed legibility and unity.

Correct
SPACING
Letters well proportioned and spaced give a feeling of rhythm and unity: the word is legible and flows.

Modern trend – very close spacing, even between verticals – curved letters touch increasing density and impact. Keep letters plain or legibility may suffer. **SPACING**

LETTER SPACING
when the space between the letters equals the width of the letters or more – but watch open letters. There must be double space between words. Ideal for condensed letters.

BRUSH LETTERS
must always be closely spaced, can even overlap.

BALLOON LETTERING: ONE-STROKE LETTERS CLOSELY SPACED WITH LEGIBLE SPACING BETWEEN THE WORDS. THE LINES ARE EQUAL DISTANCES APART AND GENERALLY ENCLOSED IN A SHAPE. PLENTY OF SPACE SHOULD SURROUND THE LETTERING.

An elementary method of spacing in a given area:
SPACING
Find centre of given area, add up letters (7) and place ½ on each side. Draw lightly one-stroke letters checking spacing before finishing. Allowances must be made for wide and narrow letters, e.g. M,W,I.

MORE˟ THAN ONE WORD
Count the no. of letters and spaces between words (18) find centre of given area and place ½ the copy on each side. Do single-stroke letters first, correct spacing, then finish. ˟There must be double the space between words, otherwise legibility suffers.

SANS SERIF (BLOCK LETTER) CAPITALS
'Helvetica' medium – a popular block typeface

Horizontals a little less in weight. Crossbars must be above centre or they appear to sag – in A placed to balance.

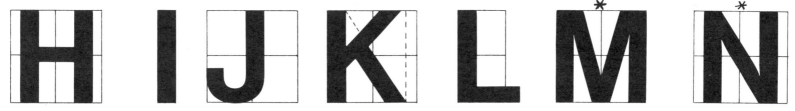

Note this line. Spacing is not mechanical it is judged by the eye. Letters balance the white spaces.

Curved letters will appear smaller unless the curves run slightly over the top and base lines.
Watch construction of B·R·S: dotted lines indicate base is a little larger than top – controls balance.

Ampersand

✱ On these letters watch construction where diagonals meet each other or verticals. Inner diagonals on M N·W little less in weight. Don't draw the squares, they are a guide with dotted lines to proportion & construction.

LOWER CASE BLOCK LETTERS
'Helvetica' medium typeface

Ascenders are short, a little less than ½ the depth between the Waist line and the Base line — except 't' and the Descenders, these are always shorter than Ascenders.

Carry all curves slightly over top and base lines. Note how the curves join *into* the straight strokes.

To check curved letters turn work upside down.

* Watch letters where curves join straight stems at top or base line — the stem cuts back slightly.

CONDENSED SANS SERIF CAPITALS

ABCDEFGHIJ

Note: all horizontals and weight around curves at top and base, a little less than the weight of the verticals.

KLMNOPQRST

Where diagonals meet each other or verticals, the top or base of the letter is drawn slightly wider than the stem.

UVWXYZ

→ Arrows indicate inner lines diminish slightly to avoid massing of colour at the junctions.

* The inner diagonals of M, N and W, must be narrower than the outside stems.

Avoid making these mistakes: **AMNWVXY** Heavy mass of colour at the junctions due to drawing all the strokes same width.

CGS Turns too short, allow too much white space inside the letter.

O Corners on curves.

D Too much curve softens the outline.

E Horizontals too heavy.

CONDENSED SANS SERIF LOWER CASE

abcdefghijklmn

*A little less weight for horizontals and top and base curves than for verticals.

opqrstuvwxyz

Where diagonals meet each other, the base is drawn slightly wider than the width of stem.

Alternative letters;

ktgry

→ Arrows indicate inner lines diminish slightly; inner diagonals of W must be narrower. Watch joining of lobe to stem, also joining of 2 stems. The curve joins *into*, not onto, the stem, and is rounded, not angular.

Avoid making these mistakes:

ace — Tops and bases all too short.

s — Top and base too short. Diagonal too long.

y — Junction of diagonal too low.

k — Diagonal too high.

k — Diagonal too low.

n — 2nd stem should curve into, not angle, onto, 1st stem.

r — Arm too long and it should curve into stem.

b — Lobe too wide and it should curve into stem.

t — Crossbar and tail too long, angle should be curve.

HEAVY EXPANDED LETTERS

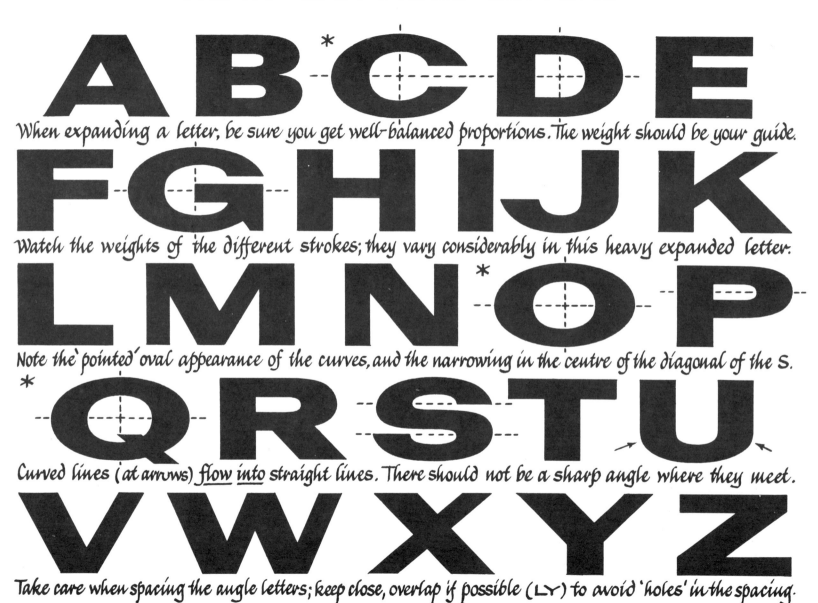

A B C D E

When expanding a letter, be sure you get well-balanced proportions. The weight should be your guide.

F G H I J K

Watch the weights of the different strokes; they vary considerably in this heavy expanded letter.

L M N O P

Note the 'pointed' oval appearance of the curves, and the narrowing in the centre of the diagonal of the S.

Q R S T U

Curved lines (at arrows) <u>flow into</u> straight lines. There should not be a sharp angle where they meet.

V W X Y Z

Take care when spacing the angle letters; keep close, overlap if possible (LY) to avoid 'holes' in the spacing.

EXPANDED LOWER CASE

a b c d e f g

Watch the inside shape of the curved letters; compare with outside shape. Note how curves join stem.

h i j k l m n

Ascenders and Descenders are short; a little less than ½ width of body, 't' is shorter. Watch tails of 'g-y'.

o p q r s t u

Where there are dotted lines watch construction carefully. × Note narrowing in centre of diagonal on 's'.

v w x y y z

Avoid making these mistakes: **a g   c o e s   b m v**

Top too large — and tail too small. Tendency to 'square' curves, and thickening of diagonal on 's'. Curves badly joined to stems. Too expanded, out of balance.

NUMERALS

Roman Light face
1234567890?

Italic
1234567890

Heavy Roman style
1234567890!?&&

Sans serif Medium
1234567890?

Condensed
1234567890?

Sans serif Heavy
1234567890 &?

Heavy Expanded
1234567890?

Brush Free style
1234567890!?&

Brush Showcard
1234567890 ?£$

SERIFS

The Serif or Finishing Stroke.

The serifs or finishing strokes were first introduced by the Romans as a method of cleaning up and making more graceful the stroke endings of their stone-cut letters. As well as beautifying the letters, serifs help the eye to pass along the line more easily. There are many variations, but whatever the letter-form, the serif used should be complimentary, and the same throughout, (e.g. condensed letters require condensed serifs), in no way altering the balance or flow of movement. The character of a letter is changed very easily by the addition of serifs; therefore they should be kept as simple as possible and drawn with extreme care.
* Note the wide variety and contrast in serifs on these Type Faces.

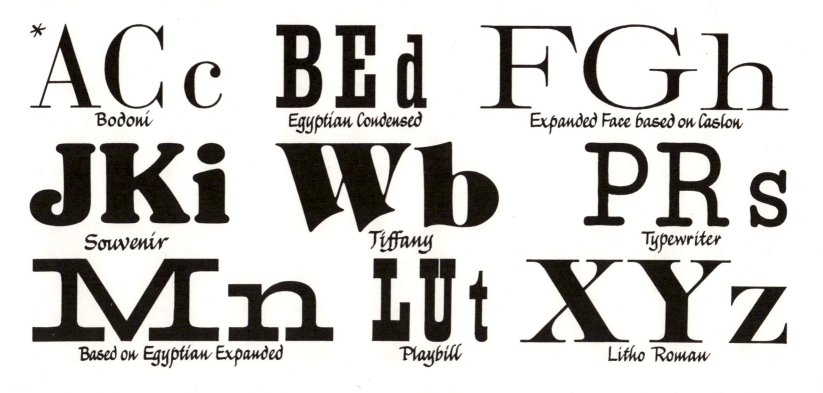

*ACc — Bodoni
BEd — Egyptian Condensed
FGh — Expanded Face based on Caslon
JKi — Souvenir
Wb — Tiffany
PRs — Typewriter
Mn — Based on Egyptian Expanded
LUt — Playbill
XYz — Litho Roman

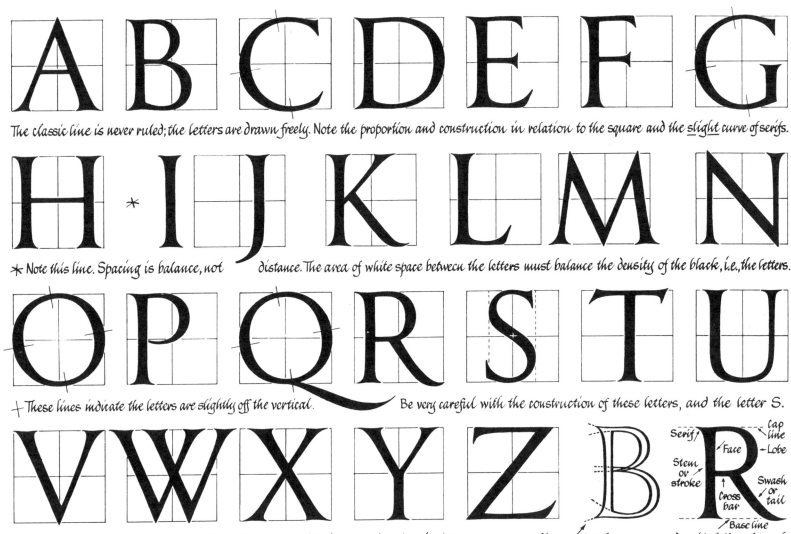

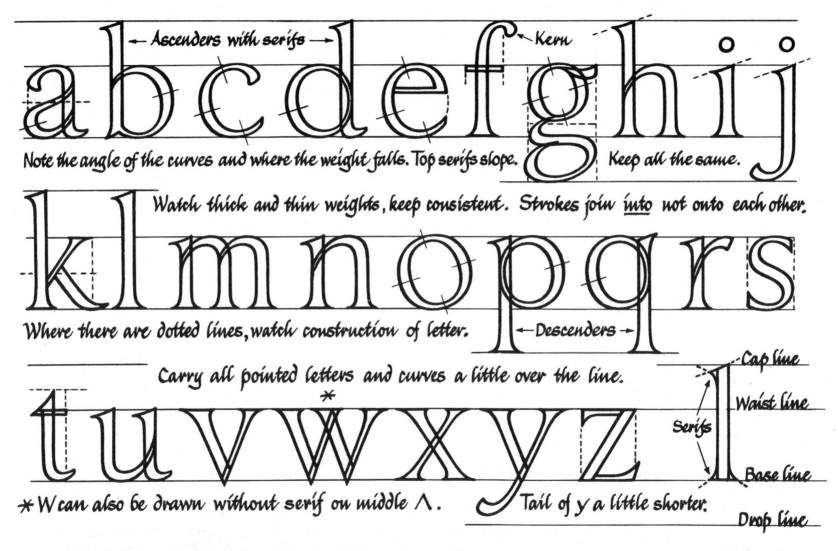

MODERN (LOWER CASE) ROMAN

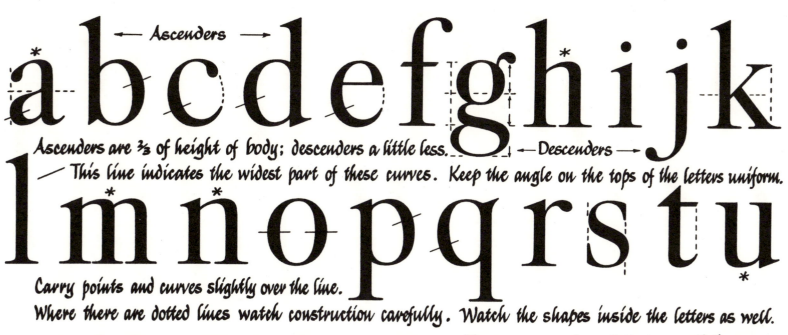

abcdefghijk

Ascenders are ⅔ of height of body; descenders a little less.

This line indicates the widest part of these curves. Keep the angle on the tops of the letters uniform.

lmnopqrstu

Carry points and curves slightly over the line.
Where there are dotted lines watch construction carefully. Watch the shapes inside the letters as well.

vwxyz

* The curves on these letters are all the same.
The kerns on A and C are exactly the same, others are the same shape but vary in weight. Weight of thins and serifs must be kept uniform.

Don't make these mistakes: Curves not uniform.   Top heavy, out of alignment.

a c e d m s t g r

Top too round belly too large. | Angles on curve tail short. | Top heavy weight centred. | Lobe incorrectly joined to stem. | 3rd stem too far away. | Centre line curve lost. | Top too heavy. | Arm too long serifs wrong.

ITALIC CAPITALS

ABCDEFGH

→ Watch carefully the join at the base of these thin horizontals. Note also the outside slope of serifs with arrows.

IJKLMNOP

Letter 'J' can also be drawn with long tail.

QRSTUVWX

YZ &   Be very careful with the slope of these letters; there could be less — but if the slope is too great, legibility will be affected.
--- Ruling guide lines will assist in keeping the slope uniform.
* Outside hairline of 'M' slopes a little more than outside heavy stroke, but be careful not to slope the hairlines of angle letters too much.

Check your work for these mistakes:

AA   B   M   R   VWXY

Being too narrow or too wide affects slope. | Top lobe too large. | 1st. hairline slopes too much. | Lobe is too wide & low. | The slope of the hairlines on these letters is too great, causing them to slope too much.

COPPERPLATE CAPITALS

Before drawing the capitals, practise these curves until you can do them in one stroke with an easy flowing movement.

These capitals are adaptable to the space available; e.g. this... or this... this... or this.
Curves must be graceful and flowing, no angles.

PEN LETTERS

Pens are stiff and awkward to use at first, but practice soon gives you the feel and control necessary to work with confidence. Begin by doing the practice strokes, followed by the simple alphabet before attempting the serif letters. The nib, square or slanting (Left slant for L.H.), must be kept clean. Paper is best to work on. The surface gives to the pen.

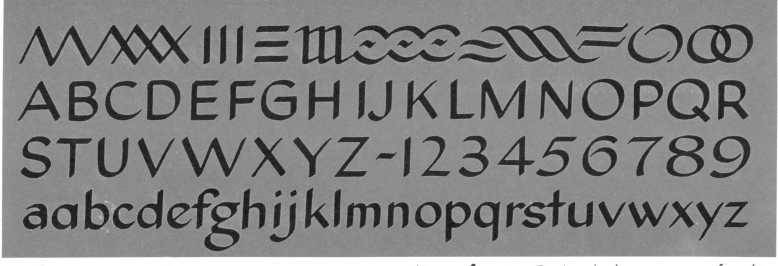

Hold the pen at a 45° angle, and draw towards you. Never push it away from you. Don't grip the pen or press heavily: this causes the nib to separate and is tiring. Let your strokes be light but deliberate. Keep the pen angle constant.

ABCDEFGHIJKLMNPQR
STUVWXYZ *Do Italic as well*
abcdefghijklmnopqrstuvwxyz

GOTHIC
also called Old English Text.

Essentially a Pen Letter and the most popular, it's chief characteristic, upright condensed angularity. The spacing must be close and even. Though highly ornamental the letters can also be simplified.

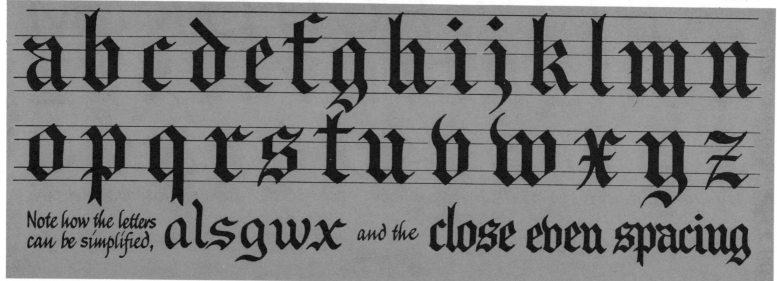

Note how the letters can be simplified, alsgwx and the close even spacing

Place tracing paper over the letters. Use a broad nib and let the pen form the letters. Do small letters first.

* The Capitals can be simplified or made more decorative by adding extra lines & flourishes.

ITALIC CAPITALS

The Simple Capitals should be mastered before adding the swashes or flourishes – slope about 9°.

Height of Capitals from 6½ to 7½ Pen widths. The numbers over the letters indicate the No. of strokes.

*Long flourishes should only be used where there is plenty of space – e.g. commencing a paragraph.

Don't make curls. They are ugly.

ITALIC WRITING

Based on the Italic Script used by Italian Scholars during the Renaissance who used only broad pens. This writing should be practised first with a broad pen or relief type of nib. Never use a pointed flexible nib.

Holding the pen lightly on a 45° angle to the writing line. First do the practice strokes until you get the feeling of evenly Controlled Angular Rhythm that is essential when doing this Italic Writing.

Practise without lines, keep the strokes even and almost upright. Should never be too sloping - about 9°

/\/\/\/\/\/\   ∩∩∩∩∩   uuuuu   ccccc   ooooo   vvvvv

a b b c d d e e f g h i j k l m n o

Body of letter is   5 Pen widths high.   Note   dashes over i j not dots.

p q r s t u v w x x y y z   * a b

* Showing the single stroke.

Ascenders and Descenders are equal to the height of Body or less, depending on the amount of space. With the exception of 'e f t x' the letters are made with one stroke commencing at the arrow.

Write each letter several times until you can remember the strokes. Speed comes with practice.

Next practise these
HORIZONTAL JOINS   oa oi oc on ox va os od fo fe ff tr tu ft tt

tram loan cod fox cocoa voice was son loss etc.

Then make up words using these joins. Some letters are better left unjoined e.g. ss st sc.

BRUSH (CARTOON) LETTERS
Use a pointed brush No.4 series 7 or 3A – Windsor & Newton

Brush Letters are drawn by a combination of strokes, straight and slightly curved giving the letters a forward movement be they vertical or slanting. Holding the brush at an angle, place the tip on the paper and with firm pressure, draw the stroke with a certain amount of speed to avoid wobbling the brush. The angle of the brush plus pressure applied determines the width of the stroke – the lower the angle the wider the stroke.

Stem strokes should be straight or slightly curved forward – never curved backwards, e.g. Note angle at ends of stroke.

Horizontals are straight or slightly curved, e.g. not this

Practise these Brush Capitals about 1" high, medium weight, on newspaper. Use paint that flows easily. Study the construction of each letter first so that you do not make the mistakes shown above.

A B C D E F G H I J K L

Arrows indicate the direction and number of strokes. First stroke commencing at the dot.

M N O P Q R S T U V

W X Y Z

POINTED MARKER & PENTEL PENS CAN ALSO BE USED FOR THIS BASIC BRUSH 'CARTOON' STYLE. SPACE TIGHTLY – LETTERS CAN TOUCH & OVERLAP.

BRUSH (CARTOON L/C) LETTERS
Use a pointed brush No 4 - or pointed Marker & Pentel pens

POINTED MARKER & PENTEL PENS ARE IDEAL FOR THIS CARTOON STYLE. KEEP PEN ANGLE LOW-WORK ON <u>SIDE</u> OF <u>POINT</u>-NOTE ENDS / SLANT. POSITION OF THE HAND CHANGES FOR HORIZONTALS / BRING TOWARDS YOU-AWAY FOR DIAGONALS.

a a b c d e e f g h i j k
l m n o p q r s t t u v
w x y y z

Arrows indicate the number and direction of the strokes, → the first stroke commencing at the dot. Note commencing and finishing angle of the strokes.

Don't make the following mistakes which produce badly balanced letters:

a — Belly is too round and it should join into, not onto, the stem, a complete oval.

a — Top too small. Belly too large and round.

c — Tail should be longer.

e — Top loop too small.

e — Misuse of crossbar.

n — 2nd stem should be the same angle as 1st stem and join into, not onto, it.

v — Base too heavy, strokes have spread too much.

When you can do the letters slanting try them upright, then try words and groups of words, but — **remember to keep the letters close together.**

COMMERCIAL SCRIPT

Generally written with a brush on Bond paper and pasted up on board. It should appear spontaneous and _must be legible_.

Brush Script is not an easy way to letter because it must be controlled yet written fairly fast otherwise it appears laboured. Therefore to do good

First check your handwriting for any restricting characteristics; always making a letter a certain way which will limit you in your styles. To avoid this, experiment with various ways of writing the same letter.

Brush Script you must—(1) Have complete control of the brush. (2) Be familiar with an able to make True Letter-Forms. (3) Have a sense of Design—(4) Have legible handwriting.

When you have done this with each letter, do the complete alphabet in the weights illustrated below. Practise on Newspaper—use a pointed brush, medium size, 3-4, and paint, which must flow off the brush. Work fairly fast.

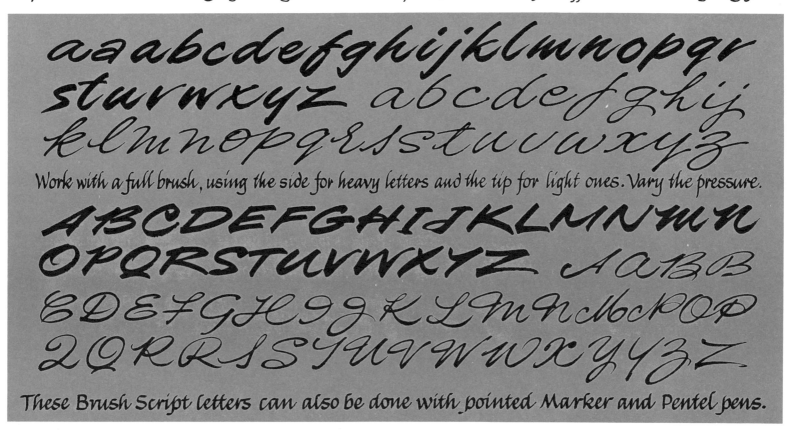

aa abcdefghijklmnopqr stuvwxyz abcdefghij klmnopqrsstuvwxyz

Work with a full brush, using the side for heavy letters and the tip for light ones. Vary the pressure.

ABCDEFGHIJKLMN OPQRSTUVWXYZ AABB CDEFGHIJKLMNOPQR 2QRRSSYUVWWXYZ

These Brush Script letters can also be done with pointed Marker and Pentel pens.

COMMERCIAL SCRIPT (2)

Before attempting to do words practise these strokes and joins. Holding the brush firmly, and working on the side, move the hand up and down along the paper. Vary the pressure, but practically no finger movement.

Practise slowly at first then gradually increase the speed, but control the movement e.g. *a* not *a*

cn mn mw ai ooc cn mn mw ai ooc
ee ee le le do ab cl hi th ja fe yr jo

Your practice should consist of leaning letters first, in light, medium, and heavy weight; followed by the same in an upright letter. Then do short words — and the now New Aim for you too etc.

control balance → of long words by writing along a pencil line. Keep the letters even. Don't stray up and down.

Broken Movement

Long words may be broken. Varying the size of the letters gives more movement.

After the Newspaper practice use thin Bond paper and ink. Do spontaneous write-outs of your name or a piece of copy until you achieve a satisfactory piece of script. Make the most of Capital Letters.

Medium weight   light   and Bold
Medium weight   very light   and Bold

DRAWING HINTS

Lettering for reproduction is usually drawn larger, half or twice up. First draw up on tissue. When satisfied with tracing rub H B pencil on the back of tissue. Then using a tracing steel, or 6H pencil, trace lettering onto board. For dark backgrounds use white crayon. Rub in well with cotton wool. Use sellotape to hold tissue in place when tracing.

Stage (1)
Tracing

Do one-stroke letters first to establish approximate spacing and width of the lettering. Correct and retrace.

Stage (2)
Tracing

Build up the letters freehand to the desired weight. This gives colour and checks spacing. Correct and retrace.

Stage (3)
Tracing

Draw the letters carefully, check width with dividers or piece of paper. Use guide lines. Rub back of tissue with pencil. Trace down.

A — Ink in by ruling straight lines with a brush or pen. 'A' has a brush ruled outline. Note how the corners kick out slightly giving a soft character to the letter.

B — 'B' has a pen ruled outline. The letter has a clean-cut mechanical look. Always build up the outline before filling in. Use white paint to clean up untidy lines.

C — Roman style letters are best drawn freehand with a fine pen. Fill in as you draw. Use short strokes. Keep the pen on inside. Turn paper for curves.

Turn lettering upside down to examine curves and the general colour. Finish inking in before correcting with white paint.

Ruling lines with a brush: Hold the brush upright with ferrule firmly against raised edge of ruler. 2nd finger rests on top of ruler. Draw the tip of brush lightly and quickly along paper. Raise the edge of ruler for each line.

A quick method for drawing 'S'

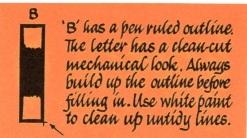

Draw 2 circles - top slightly smaller. Mark ends of letter, width at centre, top and base. Draw in rest of letter, but don't lose the curve at the centre.

DRY BRUSH The effect produced by working with very little paint on the brush.

REVERSE lettering, white on black can be done by outlining and inking around the letters, or painting white on black.

MISCELLANEOUS

ONE STROKE
A quick and easy way to indicate lettering. Mark off proportion (width) of letters with dots e.g. A¾, B½, O full — use curved sections on curved letters. Watch spacing and pencil in lightly.

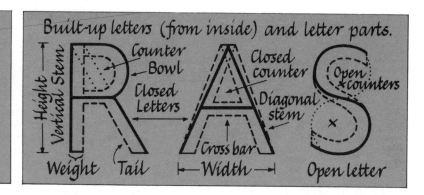
Built-up letters (from inside) and letter parts.

LIGHT FACE · MEDIUM **NORMAL · CONDENSED**
Medium weight is about 1/10 of the letter height. Letter proportions are controlled by the height.
BOLD · EXTRA BOLD **EXTENDED · *ITALIC***

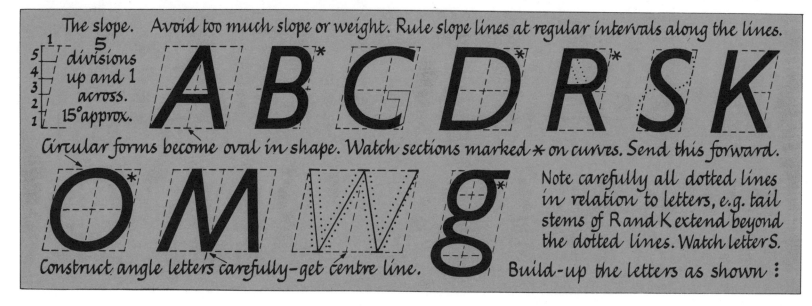

UNCIAL LETTERS

Uncials (from "uncia"-inch) are suitable for Book Jackets, Record Covers, Letterheads or Product Names.

ABCDEFGHIJKK
LMNOPQRSTTU
UVUWXYYZ ROMAN UNCIALS

abcdefghij
klmnopqrst
uvwxyz half uncials

Uncial letters are a combination of capital and lower case forms. Roman Uncials look soft and round compared with the squareness of the Irish Uncials, with their distinctive wedge-shaped serifs.

Pen slant for Roman Uncials. 30°
Wedge serifs
Pen square for Irish Uncials.

ABCDEFGHIJK
LMNOPQRSTT
UVWXYZ IRISH UNCIALS

abcdefghijk
lmnopqrstt
uvwxyz half uncials

TYPE FACES

ABCDEFGHIJKLMNOPQRSTUVWXYZabcdefghijklmnopqrstuvwxyz1234567890
BODONI ULTRA 42 POINT

ABCDEFGHIJKLMNOPQRSTUVWXYZabcdefghijklmnopqrstuvwxyz&1234567890
BEMBO 36 POINT

ABCDEFGHKabcdefghijklmnopqrstuvwxyz&
BEMBO ITALIC

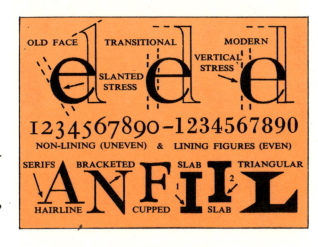

ABCDEFGHIJKLMNOPQRSTUVWXYZabcdefghijklmnopqrstuvwxyz1234567890
CLARENDON 36 POINT

TYPE FACES

A 30 POINT
SOUVENIR

ABCDEFGHIJKLMNOPQRSTUVWXYZ abcdefghijklmnopqrstuvwxyz 1234567890&!?%$

A 30 POINT
PLAYBILL

ABCDEFGHIJKLMNOPQRSTUVWXYZ & abcdefghijklmnopqrstuvwxyz 1234567890?!

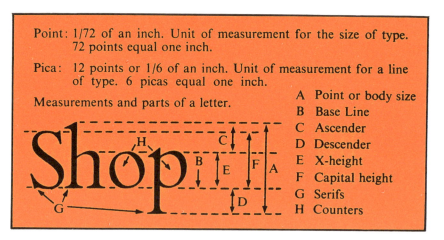

Point: 1/72 of an inch. Unit of measurement for the size of type. 72 points equal one inch.

Pica: 12 points or 1/6 of an inch. Unit of measurement for a line of type. 6 picas equal one inch.

Measurements and parts of a letter.

A Point or body size
B Base Line
C Ascender
D Descender
E X-height
F Capital height
G Serifs
H Counters

A 30 POINT
TIFFANY

ABCDEFGHIJKLMNOPQRSTUVWXYZabcdefghijklmnopqrstuvwxyz1234567890&!?%$